Fuck This Shit Show

A Guided Journal For Fully Expressed Women

Connect with us
urbanbetches.com
facebook.com/urbanbetches
Instagram: urban_betches
Pintrest: Urban Betches

First Edition December 2019
© 2019 Urban Betches
ISBN: 9781710995046
All Rights Reserved

For information about special bespoke purchases contact us at info@urbanbetches.com

Welcome

This is your time to let off some steam and be fully fucking expressed. Between these covers, you'll find the perfect page that reflects your day. So whoever or whatever has fucked you off, soothe your frustrations, your stresses and unapologetically get that shit journalled.

Life is too precious to be serious all of the time, so shine like a fucking star, laugh at yourself, laugh at life and love the people that matter the most in your world.

So hurry the fuck up and laugh and giggle your way through this journal, and write some fucking cuss words that make you feel completely and utterly expressed.

Don't keep your journal a secret, spread the word so your friends can have their own too. Let us know how much you're enjoying your journal by leaving a review on Amazon.

This journal is part of the Fully Expressed Series

Let us send you special gift to your inbox
email us at gift@urbanbetches.com

Happy Fucking Journaling
Kenzie & Chanel - The Urban Betches

Notes & Shit

date: _____ S M T W T F S

Which asshole tested my fucking patience?

Who pressed my Bitch Button today?

Important Shit

- over this
- done with this
- not taking any
- don't give a

SHIT

What bad fuckery is on my mind?

What positive shit did I achieve today?

> I THINK I'VE SEIZED THE WRONG FUCKING DAY

Today's Zen Musings...

date: _____ S M T W T F S

My fucking patience was tested when...

Who got my bitch side today?

Tomorrow's Shit List

FUCK
- You
- Me
- Off
- This
- It
- That

Today has been...

- ⭕ A ray of fucking sunshine
- ⭕ An epic shit show
- ⭕ Meh... move on
- ⭕ Fan-Fucking-Tastic
- ⭕ A monumental fuck up

> G ood
> M orning
> M other
> F uckers

Excuse me... I have some shit to say...

My redeemable quality that made me shine today

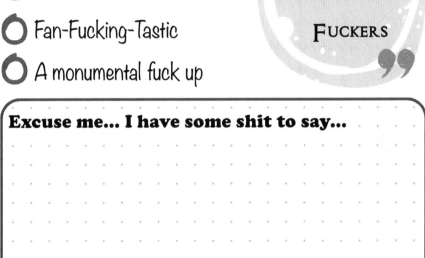

date: _____   S M T W T F S

Tomorrow I will do:
More   **Less**

☆ _____
☆ _____
☆ _____
☆ _____

> "Is fuck an emotion? Because I feel that shit in my soul"

Well that didn't go as fucking planned...

Hmm... Who made my Shit List Today?

_____
_____
_____
_____
_____
_____
_____
_____
_____

Today's favorite Cuss Word

Today's Treat Yo' Self reward is

Breathe and let go...
today's thankful moment

How did I deal with the motherfucker who pissed me off?

date: _____ S M T W T F S

Doodle some shit

Fuck
- You
- Him
- Off
- This
- It all
- This job
- That

Stuff to do when I'm not power napping

_____

_____

_____

_____

Breathe... Today's moments of gratitude

> **Holy fuckballs - is the day over yet?**

Fucking Happiness
write the words you need to hear

What shit fuckery happened today?

★ over this
★ done with this
★ not taking any
★ don't give a

SHIT

I AM

date: _____ S M T W T F S

Fucking cuss words I live by...

Shit List for another day

what's your mood?

Who got an ass kicking today?

★ over this
★ done with this
★ not taking any
★ don't give a

SHIT

Today's monumental FUCK UP was...

Today's humbling moment

Today's Zen Musings...

date: _____ S M T W T F S

How did I deal with the workplace Asshole?

What fucked me off today?

Shit I must do

FUCK
- You
- Me
- Off
- This
- It
- That

Today has been...

- ⭕ A ray of fucking sunshine
- ⭕ An epic shit show
- ⭕ Meh... move on
- ⭕ Fan-Fucking-Tastic
- ⭕ A monumental fuck up

> **Fucking proud of being weird**

Calm the fuck down... what's on my mind?

Who saved my ass today?

date: _____ Ⓢ Ⓜ Ⓣ Ⓦ Ⓣ Ⓕ Ⓢ

Tomorrow I will do:
More   **Less**

_____ ☆ _____
_____ ☆ _____
_____ ☆ _____
              ☆

> "I've been doing a lot of whatever the fuck I want lately... and I like it"

Who tested my fucking patience today?

No fucking excuses list

_____
_____
_____
_____
_____
_____
_____
_____
_____
_____

sum it up!

Who got my Fuck Off stare?

Today's Treat Yo' Self reward is

Today's little victory

What fuckery happen today?

date: _____   S M T W T F S

Fuck
- ○ You
- ○ Him
- ○ Off
- ○ This
- ○ It all
- ○ This job
- ○ That

Doodle some shit

I was so close to loosing my shit when...

_____
_____
_____
_____

Today's finest fucking moment...

> **The chill pill I took this morning appears to have been a placebo**

Fucking Happiness
write the words you need to hear

Today's shitastrophy...

★ over this
★ done with this
★ not taking any
★ don't give a

SHIT

My positive thought of the day

date: _____ S M T W T F S

Which asshole tested my fucking patience?

Important Shit

what's your mood?

Who pressed my Bitch Button today?

★ over this
★ done with this
★ not taking any
★ don't give a

SHIT

What bad fuckery is on my mind?

What positive shit did I achieve today?

> **I'M A HAPPY GO LUCK RAY OF FUCKING SUNSHINE**

Today's Zen Musings...

date: _____ S M T W T F S

My fucking patience was tested when...

Who got my bitch side today?

Tomorrow's Shit List

FUCK
- You
- Me
- Off
- This
- It
- That

Today has been...

- ⭕ A ray of fucking sunshine
- ⭕ An epic shit show
- ⭕ Meh... move on
- ⭕ Fan-Fucking-Tastic
- ⭕ A monumental fuck up

> " Onwards buttercup, there's fuckery to spread "

Excuse me... I have some shit to say...

My redeemable quality that made me shine today

date: _____   S M T W T F S

Tomorrow I will do:
More   **Less**

☆ _____
☆ _____
☆ _____
☆ _____

> " Do all things with kindness you fucker "

Well that didn't go as fucking planned...

Hmm... Who made my Shit List Today?

_____
_____
_____
_____
_____
_____
_____
_____
_____

sum it up!

Today's favorite Cuss Word

Today's Treat Yo' Self reward is

Breathe and let go... today's thankful moment

How did I deal with the motherfucker who pissed me off today?

date: _____ S M T W T F S

Doodle some shit

Fuck
- You
- Him
- Off
- This
- It all
- This job
- That

Stuff to do when I'm not power napping

_____
_____
_____
_____

Breathe... Today's moments of gratitude

> I'm not moody, I have days when I'm less inclined to put up with shit

Fucking Happiness
write the words you need to hear

What shit fuckery happened today?

★ over this
★ done with this
★ not taking any
★ don't give a

SHIT

I AM

date: _____ S M T W T F S

Fucking cuss words I live by...

Shit List for another day

what's your mood?

Who did you give an ass kicking to today?

★ over this
★ done with this
★ not taking any
★ don't give a

SHIT

Today's monumental FUCK UP was...

Today's humbling moment

> **NO BAD THOUGHTS, NOT TODAY MOTHER FUCKER**

Today's Zen Musings...

date: _____ (S) (M) (T) (W) (T) (F) (S)

How did I deal with the workplace Asshole?

What fucked me off today?

Shit I must do

FUCK
- You
- Me
- Off
- This
- It
- That

Today has been...

- ○ A ray of fucking sunshine
- ○ An epic shit show
- ○ Meh... move on
- ○ Fan-Fucking-Tastic
- ○ A monumental fuck up

> **I don't just flirt with disaster. I give it a fucking orgasm**

Calm the fuck down... what's on my mind?

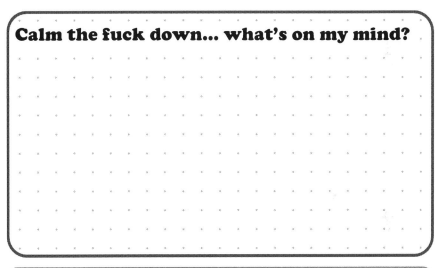

Who saved my ass today?

date: _____   S M T W T F S

Tomorrow I will do:
More   **Less**

☆ _____
☆ _____
☆ _____
☆ _____

> "PMS allows us ladies a couple of days to act like men do every freakin' day!"

Who tested my fucking patience today?

No fucking excuses list

sum it up!

Who got my Fuck Off stare?

Today's Treat Yo' Self reward is

Today's little victory

What fuckery happen today?

date: _____ S M T W T F S

Fuck:
- You
- Him
- Off
- This
- It all
- This job
- That

Doodle some shit

I was so close to loosing my shit when...

_____
_____
_____
_____

Today's finest fucking moment...

> "My only regret is that I didn't tell enough people to fuck off"

Fucking Happiness
write the words you need to hear

Today's shitastrophy...

- ★ over this
- ★ done with this
- ★ not taking any
- ★ don't give a

SHIT

My positive thought of the day

date: _____ S M T W T F S

Which asshole tested my fucking patience?

Important Shit

Who pressed my Bitch Button today?

- ★ over this
- ★ done with this
- ★ not taking any
- ★ don't give a

SHIT

What bad fuckery is on my mind?

What positive shit did I achieve today?

> **SOMETIMES A BITCH SNAPS**

Today's Zen Musings...

date: _____ S M T W T F S

My fucking patience was tested when...

Who got my bitch side today?

Tomorrow's Shit List

FUCK:
- You
- Me
- Off
- This
- It
- That

Today has been...

- ⭕ A ray of fucking sunshine
- ⭕ An epic shit show
- ⭕ Meh... move on
- ⭕ Fan-Fucking-Tastic
- ⭕ A monumental fuck up

> "EVERYBODY IS ALWAYS SO FUCKING FINE"

Excuse me... I have some shit to say...

My redeemable quality that made me shine today

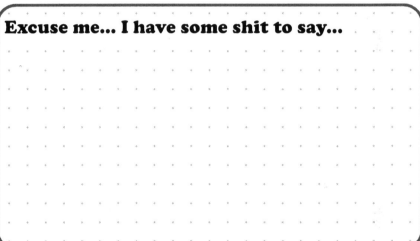

date: _____ S M T W T F S

Tomorrow I will do:
More   **Less**

_____ ☆ _____
_____ ☆ _____
_____ ☆ _____
_____ ☆ _____

> " My crystal ball says you're full of shit "

Well that didn't go as fucking planned...

Hmm... Who made my Shit List Today?

_____
_____
_____
_____
_____
_____
_____
_____
_____
_____

sum it up!

Today's favorite Cuss Word

Today's Treat Yo' Self reward is

Breathe and let go... today's thankful moment

How did I deal with the motherfucker who pissed me off today?

date: _____ S M T W T F S

Doodle some shit

Fuck
- ○ You
- ○ Him
- ○ Off
- ○ This
- ○ It all
- ○ This job
- ○ That

Stuff to do when I'm not power napping

_____

_____

_____

_____

Breathe... Today's moments of gratitude

> Women aren't moody, we simply have days where we're less inclined to put up with assholes

Fucking Happiness
write the words you need to hear

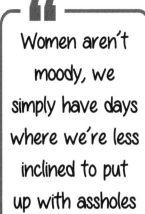

What shit fuckery happened today?

★ over this
★ done with this
★ not taking any
★ don't give a

SHIT

I AM

date: _____ S M T W T F S

Fucking cuss words I live by...

Shit List for another day

what's your mood?

Who did you give an ass kicking to today?

★ over this
★ done with this
★ not taking any
★ don't give a

SHIT

Today's monumental FUCK UP was...

Today's humbling moment

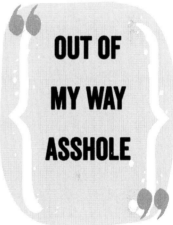

"OUT OF MY WAY ASSHOLE"

Today's Zen Musings...

date: _____ S M T W T F S

How did I deal with the workplace Asshole?

What fucked me off today?

Shit I must do

FUCK
- You
- Me
- Off
- This
- It
- That

Today has been...

- ⭕ A ray of fucking sunshine
- ⭕ An epic shit show
- ⭕ Meh... move on
- ⭕ Fan-Fucking-Tastic
- ⭕ A monumental fuck up

> **"If you don't mean what you say then shut the fuck up"**

Calm the fuck down... what's on my mind?

Who saved my ass today?

date: _____ S M T W T F S

Tomorrow I will do:
More   **Less**

☆ _____
☆ _____
☆ _____
☆ _____

> ❝ I think I'm emotionally constipated - I haven't given a shit for ages ❞

Who tested my fucking patience today?

No fucking excuses list

_____
_____
_____
_____
_____
_____
_____
_____

sum it up!

Who got my Fuck Off stare?

Today's Treat Yo' Self reward is

Today's little victory

What fuckery happen today?

date: _____   S M T W T F S

Doodle some shit

Fuck:
○ You
○ Him
○ Off
○ This
○ It all
○ This job
○ That

I was so close to loosing my shit when...

_____

_____

_____

_____

Today's finest fucking moment...

> "Oh, you think I'm cute when I'm mad? I'm about to get fucking gorgeous"

Fucking Happiness
write the words you need to hear

Today's shitastrophy...

★ over this
★ done with this
★ not taking any
★ don't give a

SHIT

My positive thought of the day

date: _____ S M T W T F S

Which asshole tested my fucking patience?

what's your mood?

Who pressed my Bitch Button today?

Important Shit

★ over this
★ done with this
★ not taking any
★ don't give a

SHIT

What bad fuckery is on my mind?

What positive shit did I achieve today?

> **DON'T LET ASSHOLES DIM YOUR FUCKING SHINE**

Today's Zen Musings...

date: _____ S M T W T F S

My fucking patience was tested when...

Who got my bitch side today?

Tomorrow's Shit List

_____
_____
_____
_____
_____
_____
_____
_____
_____
_____

FUCK
- You
- Me
- Off
- This
- It
- That

Today has been...

- ⭕ A ray of fucking sunshine
- ⭕ An epic shit show
- ⭕ Meh... move on
- ⭕ Fan-Fucking-Tastic
- ⭕ A monumental fuck up

> " I swear all the fucking time and have excellent manners "

Excuse me... I have some shit to say...

My redeemable quality that made me shine today

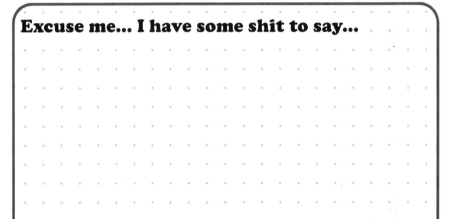

date: _____   S M T W T F S

Tomorrow I will do:
More   **Less**

_____ ☆ _____
_____ ☆ _____
_____ ☆ _____
_____ ☆ _____

> "I wish the word cunt was more socially acceptable"

Well that didn't go as fucking planned...

Hmm... Who made my Shit List Today?

_____
_____
_____
_____
_____
_____
_____
_____
_____

sum it up!

Today's favorite Cuss Word

Today's Treat Yo' Self reward is

Breathe and let go... today's thankful moment

How did I deal with the motherfucker who pissed me off today?

date: _____ S M T W T F S

Doodle some shit

Fuck
- You
- Him
- Off
- This
- It all
- This job
- That

Stuff to do when I'm not power napping

_____

_____

_____

_____

Breathe... Today's moments of gratitude

> My life might be a shit show but my hair is fabulous

Fucking Happiness
write the words you need to hear

What shit fuckery happened today?

- over this
- done with this
- not taking any
- don't give a

SHIT

I AM

date: _____ S M T W T F S

Fucking cuss words I live by...

Shit List for another day

Who did you give an ass kicking to today?

★ over this
★ done with this
★ not taking any
★ don't give a

SHIT

Today's monumental FUCK UP was…

Today's humbling moment

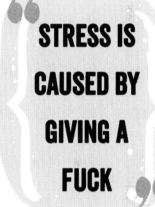

> **STRESS IS CAUSED BY GIVING A FUCK**

Today's Zen Musings…

date: _____ S M T W T F S

How did I deal with the workplace Asshole?

What fucked me off today?

Shit I must do

_____
_____
_____
_____
_____
_____
_____
_____
_____
_____

FUCK
- You
- Me
- Off
- This
- It
- That

Today has been...

- ⭕ A ray of fucking sunshine
- ⭕ An epic shit show
- ⭕ Meh... move on
- ⭕ Fan-Fucking-Tastic
- ⭕ A monumental fuck up

"Shit's about to get fancy"

Calm the fuck down... what's on my mind?

Who saved my ass today?

date: _____ S M T W T F S

Tomorrow I will do:
More   **Less**

_____ ☆ _____
_____ ☆ _____
_____ ☆ _____
_____ ☆ _____

> " The lack of swearing makes me feel fucking uncomfortable "

Who tested my fucking patience today?

No fucking excuses list

sum it up!

Who got my Fuck Off stare?

Today's Treat Yo' Self reward is

Today's little victory

What fuckery happen today?

date: _____ S M T W T F S

Doodle some shit

Fuck:
○ You
○ Him
○ Off
○ This
○ It all
○ This job
○ That

I was so close to loosing my shit when...

_____

_____

_____

_____

Today's finest fucking moment...

> Be kind and generous to yourself and tell all others to fuck off

Fucking Happiness
write the words you need to hear

Today's shitastrophy...

★ over this
★ done with this
★ not taking any
★ don't give a

SHIT

My positive thought of the day

date: _____ S M T W T F S

Which asshole tested my fucking patience?

Who pressed my Bitch Button today?

Important Shit

- over this
- done with this
- not taking any
- don't give a

SHIT

What bad fuckery is on my mind?

What positive shit did I achieve today?

> # HOLY SHIT LOOK AT ALL THOSE FUCKTARDS

Today's Zen Musings...

date: _____ S M T W T F S

My fucking patience was tested when...

Who got my bitch side today?

Tomorrow's Shit List

_____
_____
_____
_____
_____
_____
_____
_____
_____
_____

FUCK
- You
- Me
- Off
- This
- It
- That

Today has been...

- ⭕ A ray of fucking sunshine
- ⭕ An epic shit show
- ⭕ Meh... move on
- ⭕ Fan-Fucking-Tastic
- ⭕ A monumental fuck up

> A DASH OF FUCK IT AND A SPLASH OF FUCK OFF

Excuse me... I have some shit to say...

My redeemable quality that made me shine today

date: _____   S M T W T F S

Tomorrow I will do:
More **Less**

☆ _____
☆ _____
☆ _____
☆ _____

> "Don't make me flip my bitch switch"

Well that didn't go as fucking planned...

Hmm... Who made my Shit List Today?

sum it up!

Today's favorite Cuss Word

Today's Treat Yo' Self reward is

Breathe and let go... today's thankful moment

How did I deal with the motherfucker who pissed me off today?

date: _____ S M T W T F S

Fuck
- You
- Him
- Off
- This
- It all
- This job
- That

Doodle some shit

Stuff to do when I'm not power napping

_____
_____
_____
_____

Breathe... Today's moments of gratitude

> Quick question: Is it "for fucks sake" or "for fuck sake"? It's for work, so I want to make sure this email sounds professional

Fucking Happiness
write the words you need to hear

What shit fuckery happened today?

- over this
- done with this
- not taking any
- don't give a

SHIT

I AM

date: _____ S M T W T F S

Fucking cuss words I live by...

Shit List for another day

what's your mood?

Who did you give an ass kicking to today?

★ over this
★ done with this
★ not taking any
★ don't give a

SHIT

Today's monumental FUCK UP was...

Today's humbling moment

> GO FOR IT -
> TELL
> SOMEONE TO
> FUCK OFF

Today's Zen Musings...

date: _____ S M T W T F S

How did I deal with the workplace Asshole?

What fucked me off today?

Shit I must do

FUCK
- You
- Me
- Off
- This
- It
- That

Today has been...

- ◯ A ray of fucking sunshine
- ◯ An epic shit show
- ◯ Meh... move on
- ◯ Fan-Fucking-Tastic
- ◯ A monumental fuck up

" Belly laugh today - tell a betch to go and fuck off "

Calm the fuck down... what's on my mind?

Who saved my ass today?

date: _____   S M T W T F S

Tomorrow I will do:
More   **Less**

☆ ————————————
☆ ————————————
☆ ————————————
☆ ————————————

> " Dance like everyone else can go fuck themselves "

Who tested my fucking patience today?

No fucking excuses list

_____
_____
_____
_____
_____
_____
_____
_____
_____

sum it up!

Who got my Fuck Off stare?

Today's Treat Yo' Self reward is

Today's little victory

What fuckery happen today?

date: _____ S M T W T F S

Doodle some shit

Fuck
- You
- Him
- Off
- This
- It all
- This job
- That

I was so close to loosing my shit when...

Today's finest fucking moment...

> **I need someone that can handle my shit**

Fucking Happiness
write the words you need to hear

Today's shitastrophy...

- ★ over this
- ★ done with this
- ★ not taking any
- ★ don't give a

SHIT

My positive thought of the day

date: _____ S M T W T F S

Which asshole tested my fucking patience?

Who pressed my Bitch Button today?

Important Shit

- over this
- done with this
- not taking any
- don't give a

SHIT

What bad fuckery is on my mind?

What positive shit did I achieve today?

> REACH FOR THE FUCKING STARS

Today's Zen Musings...

date: _____ S M T W T F S

My fucking patience was tested when...

Who got my bitch side today?

Tomorrow's Shit List

FUCK
- You
- Me
- Off
- This
- It
- That

Today has been...

- ⭕ A ray of fucking sunshine
- ⭕ An epic shit show
- ⭕ Meh... move on
- ⭕ Fan-Fucking-Tastic
- ⭕ A monumental fuck up

> " Never under estimate the power of cuss words "

Excuse me... I have some shit to say...

My redeemable quality that made me shine today

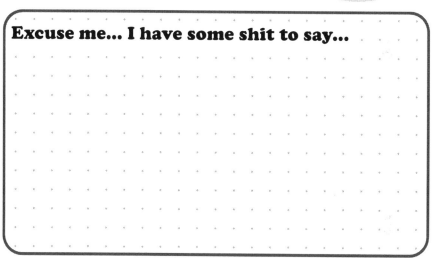

date: _____ S M T W T F S

Tomorrow I will do:
More   **Less**

☆ _____
☆ _____
☆ _____
☆ _____

> **"It's time to kick ass NOW!"**

Well that didn't go as fucking planned...

Hmm... Who made my Shit List Today?

_____
_____
_____
_____
_____
_____
_____
_____
_____

Today's favorite Cuss Word

Today's Treat Yo' Self reward is

Breathe and let go...
today's thankful moment

How did I deal with the motherfucker who pissed me off today?

date: _____   S M T W T F S

Doodle some shit

Fuck
- You
- Him
- Off
- This
- It all
- This job
- That

Stuff to do when I'm not power napping

_____
_____
_____
_____

Breathe... Today's moments of gratitude

> Life is better when you can say motherfucker

Fucking Happiness
write the words you need to hear

What shit fuckery happened today?

- over this
- done with this
- not taking any
- don't give a

SHIT

I AM

date: _____ S M T W T F S

Fucking cuss words I live by...

Shit List for another day

what's your mood?

Who did you give an ass kicking to today?

★ over this
★ done with this
★ not taking any
★ don't give a

SHIT

Today's monumental FUCK UP was...

Today's humbling moment

BITCHES GET STUFF DONE

Today's Zen Musings...

date: _____ S M T W T F S

How did I deal with the workplace Asshole?

What fucked me off today?

Shit I must do

FUCK
- You
- Me
- Off
- This
- It
- That

Today has been...

- ○ A ray of fucking sunshine
- ○ An epic shit show
- ○ Meh... move on
- ○ Fan-Fucking-Tastic
- ○ A monumental fuck up

" Mama needs a mother-fucking nap "

Calm the fuck down... what's on my mind?

Who saved my ass today?

date: _____ S M T W T F S

Tomorrow I will do:
More   **Less**

☆ _____
☆ _____
☆ _____
☆ _____

> "Herbal fucking remedies - because it's been one of those days"

Who tested my fucking patience today?

No fucking excuses list
_____
_____
_____
_____
_____
_____
_____
_____
_____
_____

sum it up!

Who got my Fuck Off stare?

Today's Treat Yo' Self reward is

Today's little victory

What fuckery happen today?

date: _____ S M T W T F S

Doodle some shit

Fuck
- ○ You
- ○ Him
- ○ Off
- ○ This
- ○ It all
- ○ This job
- ○ That

I was so close to loosing my shit when...

_____
_____
_____
_____

Today's finest fucking moment...

> I'm a smart sassy lady who likes to say Fuck a lot

Fucking Happiness
write the words you need to hear

Today's shitastrophy...

⭐ over this
⭐ done with this
⭐ not taking any
⭐ don't give a

SHIT

My positive thought of the day

date: _____ S M T W T F S

Which asshole tested my fucking patience?

Who pressed my Bitch Button today?

Important Shit

- over this
- done with this
- not taking any
- don't give a

SHIT

What bad fuckery is on my mind?

What positive shit did I achieve today?

> **FUCK OFF...**
>
> **SORRY**
>
> **I MEAN**
>
> **GOOD MORNING**

Today's Zen Musings...

date: _____ S M T W T F S

My fucking patience was tested when...

Who got my bitch side today?

Tomorrow's Shit List

FUCK
- You
- Me
- Off
- This
- It
- That

Today has been...

- ◯ A ray of fucking sunshine
- ◯ An epic shit show
- ◯ Meh... move on
- ◯ Fan-Fucking-Tastic
- ◯ A monumental fuck up

> **I will not keep calm and you can fuck off**

Excuse me... I have some shit to say...

My redeemable quality that made me shine today

date: _____   S M T W T F S

Tomorrow I will do:
More   **Less**

☆
☆
☆
☆

"Express your fucking shit"

Well that didn't go as fucking planned...

Hmm... Who made my Shit List Today?

sum it up!

Today's favorite Cuss Word

Today's Treat Yo' Self reward is

Breathe and let go... today's thankful moment

How did I deal with the motherfucker who pissed me off today?

date: _____ S M T W T F S

Doodle some shit

Fuck
- You
- Him
- Off
- This
- It all
- This job
- That

Stuff to do when I'm not power napping

_____

_____

_____

_____

Breathe... Today's moments of gratitude

> Let's keep the Dumbfuckery to a minimum today

Fucking Happiness
write the words you need to hear

What shit fuckery happened today?

- over this
- done with this
- not taking any
- don't give a

SHIT

I AM

date: _____ S M T W T F S

Fucking cuss words I live by...

Shit List for another day

what's your mood?

Who did you give an ass kicking to today?

★ over this
★ done with this
★ not taking any
★ don't give a

SHIT

Today's monumental FUCK UP was...

Today's humbling moment

> **DON'T FUCKING TOUCH ME**

Today's Zen Musings...

date: _____ S M T W T F S

How did I deal with the workplace Asshole?

What fucked me off today?

Shit I must do

FUCK
- You
- Me
- Off
- This
- It
- That

Today has been...

- ◯ A ray of fucking sunshine
- ◯ An epic shit show
- ◯ Meh... move on
- ◯ Fan-Fucking-Tastic
- ◯ A monumental fuck up

> " I'm not feeling very chatty today – off you fuck "

Calm the fuck down... what's on my mind?

Who saved my ass today?

date: _____ S M T W T F S

Tomorrow I will do:

More   **Less**

_____ ☆ _____
_____ ☆ _____
_____ ☆ _____
_____ ☆ _____

> When you feel good, you feel like taking fucking action

Who tested my fucking patience today?

No fucking excuses list

Who got my Fuck Off stare?

Today's little victory

Today's Treat Yo' Self reward is

What fuckery happen today?

date: _____ S M T W T F S

Doodle some shit

Fuck
- You
- Him
- Off
- This
- It all
- This job
- That

I was so close to loosing my shit when...

_____
_____
_____
_____

Today's finest fucking moment...

> "I like pretty things and the word **Fuck**"

Fucking Happiness
write the words you need to hear

Today's shitastrophy...

★ over this
★ done with this
★ not taking any
★ don't give a

SHIT

My positive thought of the day

date: _____ S M T W T F S

Which asshole tested my fucking patience?

Who pressed my Bitch Button today?

Important Shit

- over this
- done with this
- not taking any
- don't give a

SHIT

What bad fuckery is on my mind?

What positive shit did I achieve today?

> DO I LOOK LIKE A FUCKING PEOPLE PERSON?

Today's Zen Musings...

date: _____ S M T W T F S

My fucking patience was tested when...

Who got my bitch side today?

Tomorrow's Shit List

_____
_____
_____
_____
_____
_____
_____
_____
_____
_____

FUCK
- You
- Me
- Off
- This
- It
- That

Today has been...

- ⭕ A ray of fucking sunshine
- ⭕ An epic shit show
- ⭕ Meh... move on
- ⭕ Fan-Fucking-Tastic
- ⭕ A monumental fuck up

> " **N**AMASTE THE FUCK AWAY FROM ME "

Excuse me... I have some shit to say...

My redeemable quality that made me shine today

date: _____   S M T W T F S

Tomorrow I will do:

More   **Less**

_____ ☆ _____

_____ ☆ _____

_____ ☆ _____

_____ ☆ _____

"Smart as fuck"

Well that didn't go as fucking planned...

Hmm... Who made my Shit List Today?

_____

_____

_____

_____

_____

_____

_____

_____

_____

sum it up!

Today's favorite Cuss Word

Today's Treat Yo' Self reward is

Breathe and let go... today's thankful moment

How did I deal with the motherfucker who pissed me off today?

date: _____ Ⓢ Ⓜ Ⓣ Ⓦ Ⓣ Ⓕ Ⓢ

Fuck
- ⭘ You
- ⭘ Him
- ⭘ Off
- ⭘ This
- ⭘ It all
- ⭘ This job
- ⭘ That

Doodle some shit

Stuff to do when I'm not power napping

_____

_____

_____

_____

Breathe... Today's moments of gratitude

> "I have the power within me to be a fucking bitch"

Fucking Happiness
write the words you need to hear

What shit fuckery happened today?

★ over this
★ done with this
★ not taking any
★ don't give a

SHIT

I AM

date: _____ S M T W T F S

Fucking cuss words I live by...

Shit List for another day

what's your mood?

Who did you give an ass kicking to today?

★ over this
★ done with this
★ not taking any
★ don't give a

SHIT

Today's monumental FUCK UP was...

Today's humbling moment

> I HAVE A LIFE OF FUCKS AND FLOWS

Today's Zen Musings...

date: _____ S M T W T F S

How did I deal with the workplace Asshole?

What fucked me off today?

Shit I must do

_____
_____
_____
_____
_____
_____
_____
_____
_____
_____

FUCK
- You
- Me
- Off
- This
- It
- That

Today has been...

- ◯ A ray of fucking sunshine
- ◯ An epic shit show
- ◯ Meh... move on
- ◯ Fan-Fucking-Tastic
- ◯ A monumental fuck up

" Don't fuck with me motherfucker "

Calm the fuck down... what's on my mind?

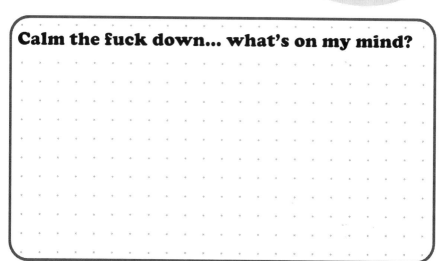

Who saved my ass today?

date: _____   S M T W T F S

Tomorrow I will do:
More   **Less**

☆ _____
☆ _____
☆ _____
☆ _____

> **Who is fucking awesome? I am**

Who tested my fucking patience today?

No fucking excuses list

sum it up!

Who got my Fuck Off stare?

Today's Treat Yo' Self reward is

Today's little victory

What fuckery happen today?

date: _____ S M T W T F S

Doodle some shit

Fuck:
- You
- Him
- Off
- This
- It all
- This job
- That

I was so close to loosing my shit when...

_____
_____
_____
_____

Today's finest fucking moment...

> **I have a constant and dependable list of cuss words**

Fucking Happiness
write the words
you need to hear

Today's shitastrophy...

★ over this
★ done with this
★ not taking any
★ don't give a

SHIT

My positive thought
of the day

date: _____ S M T W T F S

Which asshole tested my fucking patience?

Who pressed my Bitch Button today?

Important Shit

★ over this
★ done with this
★ not taking any
★ don't give a

SHIT

What bad fuckery is on my mind?

What positive shit did I achieve today?

> TODAY IS GOING TO FUCKING AWESOME

Today's Zen Musings...

date: _____ S M T W T F S

My fucking patience was tested when…

Who got my bitch side today?

Tomorrow's Shit List

FUCK
- You
- Me
- Off
- This
- It
- That

Today has been...

- ⭕ A ray of fucking sunshine
- ⭕ An epic shit show
- ⭕ Meh... move on
- ⭕ Fan-Fucking-Tastic
- ⭕ A monumental fuck up

> **Step into the spotlight Rockstar - It's your time**

Excuse me... I have some shit to say...

My redeemable quality that made me shine today

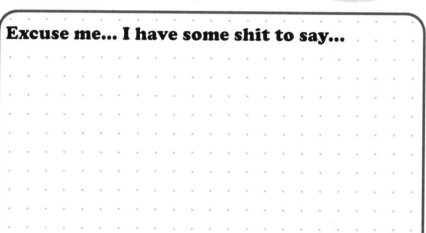

date: _____ Ⓢ Ⓜ Ⓣ Ⓦ Ⓣ Ⓕ Ⓢ

Tomorrow I will do:
More   **Less**

_____ ☆ _____
_____ ☆ _____
_____ ☆ _____
_____ ☆ _____

> " Talented motherfucker "

Well that didn't go as fucking planned...

Hmm... Who made my Shit List Today?

sum it up!

Today's favorite Cuss Word

Today's Treat Yo' Self reward is

Breathe and let go... today's thankful moment

How did I deal with the motherfucker who pissed me off today?

date: _____ S M T W T F S

Doodle some shit

Fuck
- You
- Him
- Off
- This
- It all
- This job
- That

Stuff to do when I'm not power napping

_____
_____
_____
_____

Breathe... Today's moments of gratitude

> **Be smart with your fucks**

Fucking Happiness
write the words you need to hear

What shit fuckery happened today?

- over this
- done with this
- not taking any
- don't give a

SHIT

I AM

date: _____ S M T W T F S

Fucking cuss words I live by...

Shit List for another day

what's your mood?

Who did you give an ass kicking to today?

★ over this
★ done with this
★ not taking any
★ don't give a

SHIT

Today's monumental FUCK UP was...

Today's humbling moment

> **GET YOU FUCKING HAPPY ON**

Today's Zen Musings...

date: _____ S M T W T F S

How did I deal with the workplace Asshole?

What fucked me off today?

Shit I must do

_____
_____
_____
_____
_____
_____
_____
_____
_____
_____

FUCK
- You
- Me
- Off
- This
- It
- That

Today has been...

- ⭕ A ray of fucking sunshine
- ⭕ An epic shit show
- ⭕ Meh... move on
- ⭕ Fan-Fucking-Tastic
- ⭕ A monumental fuck up

> **Make fucking magic happen**

Calm the fuck down... what's on my mind?

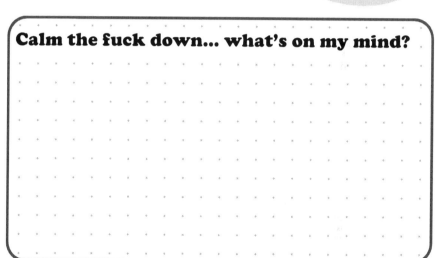

Who saved my ass today?

date: _____   S M T W T F S

Tomorrow I will do:

More   **Less**

☆
☆
☆
☆

> **Aww... my middle finger likes you**

Who tested my fucking patience today?

No fucking excuses list

Who got my Fuck Off stare?

Today's Treat Yo' Self reward is

Today's little victory

What fuckery happen today?

date: _____ S M T W T F S

Doodle some shit

Fuck
- You
- Him
- Off
- This
- It all
- This job
- That

I was so close to loosing my shit when...

_____

_____

_____

_____

Today's finest fucking moment...

> **Cussing like a fucking lady**

Fucking Happiness
write the words you need to hear

Today's shitastrophy...

- over this
- done with this
- not taking any
- don't give a

SHIT

My positive thought of the day

date: _____ S M T W T F S

Which asshole tested my fucking patience?

Important Shit

Who pressed my Bitch Button today?

- over this
- done with this
- not taking any
- don't give a

SHIT

What bad fuckery is on my mind?

What positive shit did I achieve today?

> **DO NO HARM BUT TAKE NO SHIT**

Today's Zen Musings...

Printed in Great Britain
by Amazon